W O R L D   O F   W O N D E R

Published by Creative Education
123 South Broad Street
Mankato, Minnesota 56001

Creative Education is an imprint of
The Creative Company.

Art direction by Rita Marshall
Design by The Design Lab

Photographs by Corbis (Stuart Westmorland), The
Image Finders (Kenny Bahr, Jim Baron, Rob Curtis/The
Early Birders, David Haas, Werner Lobert, Mark & Sue
Werner), JLM Visuals (Don Blegen, Richard P. Jacobs,
Breck P. Kent, Alex Kerstitch, Marypat Zitzer), KAC
Productions (Kathy Adams Clark, Larry Ditto, Peter
Gottschling, Greg W. Lasley, John & Gloria Tveten),
Steve Maslowski, George Robbins

Library of Congress Cataloging-in-Publication Data

Hoff, Mary King.
Migration / by Mary Hoff.
p. cm. — (World of wonder)
Summary: Discusses animal migration, including
different animals that migrate, the routes they take
and how they navigate, and the various reasons
that they make the journey.
ISBN 1-58341-241-7
1. Animal migration—Juvenile literature. [1. Animals—
Migration.] I. Title.

QL754 .H64 2002
591.56'8—dc21   2002017446

First Edition

9 8 7 6 5 4 3 2 1

cover & page 1: an arctic tern
page 2: ruddy turnstones
page 3: a humpback whale

Creative Education presents

WORLD OF WONDER

MIGRATION

BY MARY HOFF

Birds that fly thousands of miles without resting 🕷 Fish that return after years away to the stream in which they hatched 🐺 Deer that travel uphill and down again ⚡ The world is full of living things that migrate, or journey from one place to another and back again.

🌍

MIGRATION IS AN IMPORTANT adaptation for many animals. Some migrate to avoid harsh weather. Others migrate to take advantage of abundant food. And yet others migrate to provide their young with the special conditions they need to grow and thrive.

Butterflies migrate to escape cold weather

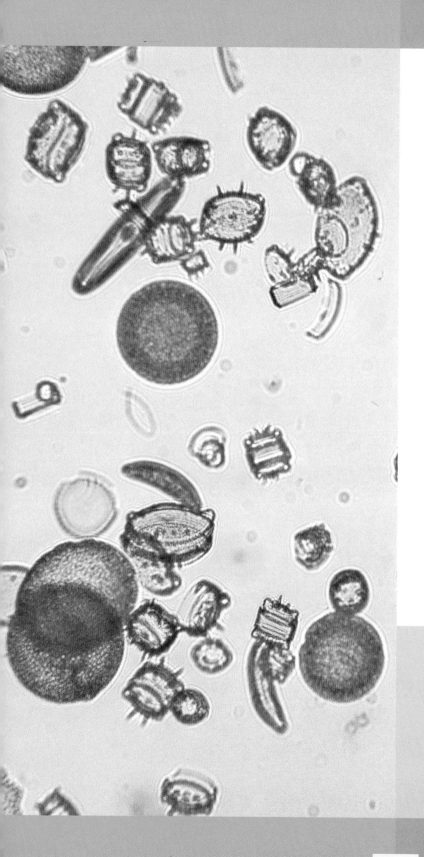

DAILY DEEDS

The ocean is home to millions upon millions of tiny creatures called zooplankton. Each night, the **zooplankton** rise to the surface of the ocean to feed on **phytoplankton**. When day comes, the zooplankton travel back down below the surface.

☀ Daily, repeating movements such as this one are called diel migrations. By heading below

NATURE NOTE: *The name "zooplankton" comes from Greek words meaning "wandering animal." Zooplankton drift about the ocean with the currents.*

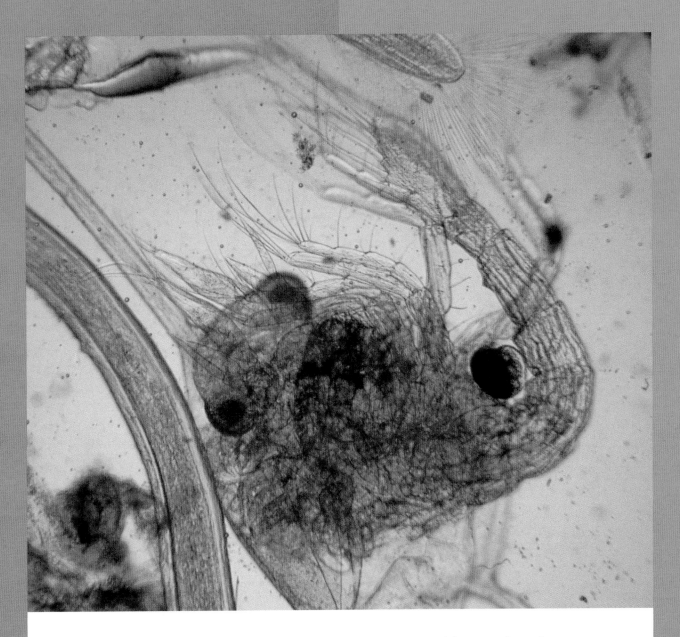

the surface during the daytime, the zooplankton avoid heat and predators. By coming back up at night when it's safer, they are able to take advantage of the rich supply of phytoplankton that live at the surface.

Zooplankton migrate daily for food

BIRD JOURNEYS

Each fall, some 10 billion birds fly from northern America, Europe, and Asia to winter homes in the south. When spring comes, they travel north again, often to the same neighborhood they left. Some birds in the southern **hemisphere** do just the opposite. They travel north in the fall and south in the spring.

NATURE NOTE: *More than 200 species of birds migrate from the United States to southern destinations each fall.*

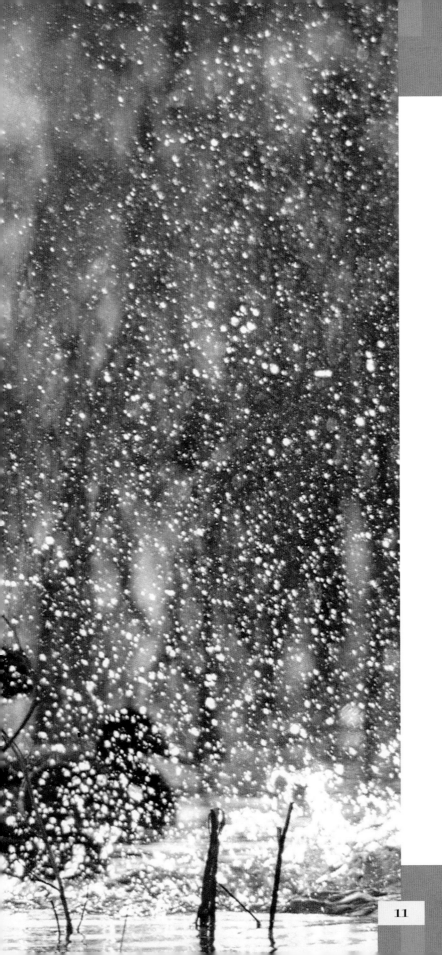

❄ Why do birds make this amazing trip? Their summer homes can provide food and shelter during the growing season. But as winter approaches, it becomes cold and harder to find food. So they travel to a place where their food is still growing or flying, crawling, or swimming about.

❋ Some birds, including eagles, swallows, and ducks, migrate during the day. Others, such as warblers and robins, migrate at night. Night travel lessens the chance of being

Mallard ducks prefer daytime migrations

NATURE NOTE: *Not all birds migrate by flying. Some penguins and auks (a seabird that lives north of the equator) swim to their destinations. Ostriches walk.*

eaten. It also lets insect-eating birds use the daytime, when insects are active, to refuel.

Not all migrating birds migrate north and south. Some migrate up mountainsides for the summer and down for the winter. In areas that have been logged, the blue grouse of western North America does the opposite. It summers in mountain valleys, where berries and insects are plentiful. In the fall, it travels to the forests higher in the mountains, where it lives on tree buds until spring.

BUTTER-FLIGHT

Like bright orange flowers floating through the sky, monarch butterflies head south each fall from the northern United States. Some go to Florida, California, or Texas. Others travel to Mexico—a total distance of 2,000 miles (3,200 km) or more. They are unusual migrators because they lay eggs in the southern United States on the return trip, so the butterflies that return north are not the same ones that left. But because they are the same species, this movement is still considered migration.

🕷 Other insects migrate, too. The bath white butterfly travels across the Pyrenees Mountains between Spain and France. The convolvulus hawk moth flies from northern Europe to the Mediterranean Sea. Painted lady butterflies fly from northern Europe to the Sahara Desert in northern Africa. Bogong

NATURE NOTE: *Monarchs fly up to 80 miles (129 km) per day during their migrations.*

14

NATURE NOTE: *Monarchs sometimes get swept off course during migration and end up in Europe by accident.*

Painted lady butterflies are strong fliers

moths spend the spring as caterpillars in the grasslands of Australia. After they undergo **metamorphosis**, the adult moths travel to higher land in the Australian Alps.

BACK FOR BABIES

Many animals migrate to special spots to lay their eggs. Tree frogs live in trees—not a very good place for tadpoles. When it comes time to lay eggs, they migrate to swamps or ponds, which provide the water their young need.

Tree frogs leave the trees to lay eggs in water

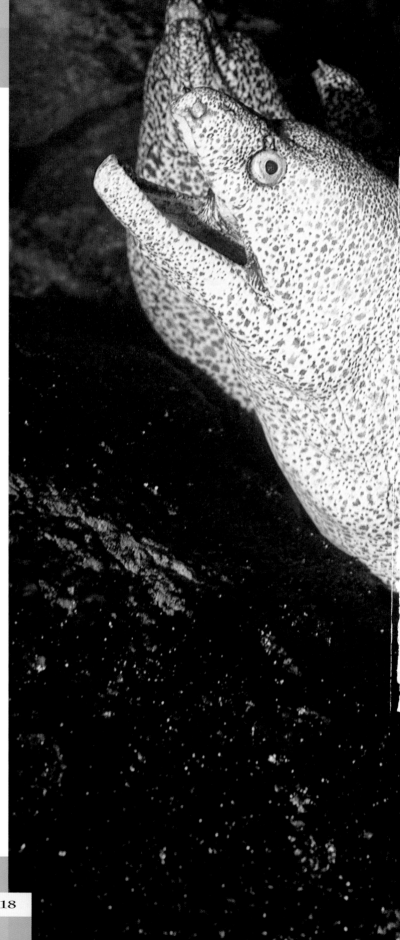

Common eels lay their eggs in the Sargasso Sea, a seaweed-filled area in the Atlantic Ocean. In the spring, the tiny eel **larvae** begin a long journey—some travel to North America, and some go to Europe. When they reach rivers that empty into the ocean, many eels swim up the rivers and live there until they are about 8 to 10 years old. Then they swim back to the Sargasso Sea, where they lay their eggs, starting the cycle over again.

Green sea turtles leave the

eastern coast of South America each December to travel to Ascension Island, more than 1,300 miles (2,090 km) away. There, they mate and lay their eggs, then return home. The young are able to find their way

NATURE NOTE: *Some eels travel 3,500 miles (5,645 km) or more to get to the Sargasso Sea to lay their eggs.*

Eels are known for their distant migrations

to South America on their own after they hatch—and return to Ascension Island 15 or more years later, when they are old enough to reproduce.

❋ Salmon lay their eggs in rivers. When the young hatch, they travel downstream and out to sea, where they spend several years. When they are mature, they travel back to the same river to lay their own eggs.

NATURE NOTE: *People build special structures called "fish ladders" to help salmon migrate past dams in rivers.*

A green sea turtle crawls ashore to lay eggs

FLIPPER TRIPS

Each fall, huge humpback whales travel thousands of miles from their ocean homes near the north and south poles to warmer waters close to the equator. Whales that summer in the far North travel to the coast of Africa, Mexico, the Hawaiian Islands, or the West Indies. Those that live in the southern hemisphere travel to the waters along the coasts of southern continents.

🚢 Other whales, including gray whales, blue whales, and orcas (killer

Humpback whales migrate biannually

whales), also migrate. Why do whales make this journey? No one knows for sure. One likely reason is to find warmer water for their babies.

Seals migrate, too. Alaskan fur seals spend summers in the far North, where Alaska and Russia almost meet. In the fall, the mothers and their pups go south—some migrating to Japan, others to the California coast. The males stay near Alaska year-round. They are reunited in the spring when the long-distance travelers return.

BEASTS AND BATS

Large-antlered deer called caribou spend summers eating **lichens** on the **tundra** in Alaska. In the winter, they travel to forests, where they find food and shelter from harsh weather. Other four-footed plant-eaters that migrate include the saiga antelope of Russia and the wildebeest of Africa. These animals migrate to find good food supplies. Mule deer and elk, found in western North America, both live in the mountains in the summer and move to lower land, where there is less snow and more available food, in the winter.

Some bats migrate to make sure they have a good food supply throughout the year. The Mexican free-tailed bat journeys all the way from Oregon to southern Mexico. Other migrating bats include the little brown bat and the red bat.

NATURE NOTE: *The air that gets trapped in their hollow hairs helps caribou stay afloat when they swim across rivers during migration.*

Elk move to lower elevations in the fall

GETTING READY

Animals that travel far must fuel up their bodies for the journey, just as people put gas in their cars before they set out on a long trip. For example, birds eat more food in the fall and spring, adding a layer of fat that will provide the energy they need during their migration.

How do migrators know when it's almost time to leave? Some pay attention to the changes in their surroundings—for instance, the arrival of cold or dry weather. The clue

that tells birds to prepare for migration is the amount of time between sunrise and sunset. In the fall, days get shorter and nights grow longer. This change causes birds that migrate to get restless and to eat more. They add layer upon layer of fat to their bodies, storing the energy they will need for the long flight ahead.

NATURE NOTE: *The blackpoll warbler fattens from one-third of an ounce (9 g) to three-quarters of an ounce (21 g) before it leaves New England to fly to South America.*

Birds fatten themselves up before migrating

WHERE NOW?

How do animals know which way to go when they migrate? The position of the sun and the stars provide important **navigation** clues for many migrators. But because the sun and the stars can be hidden by clouds, migrators need other clues, too. Some follow rivers, coastlines, or other land features. Some can also use the earth's **magnetic field** to tell which way is which. Dolphins, honeybees, tuna, turtles, bacteria, and birds can all sense Earth's magnetic field.

Salmon use scents to find their way home. Each stream smells a little different. They remember the fragrance of the stream in which they grew up and return there to start the next generation.

Other clues include changes in temperature and moisture. Ocean animals may use currents to tell which way is which. Some animals learn the way from their elders. Often, migrating animals use a combination of clues. For example, green sea turtles may use currents, the sun, stars, and odors to find their way to their breeding grounds and back.

MANY WAYS TO GO

From eels that slip through the ocean to deer that head for the hills, many animals migrate to survive the changing challenges of life. Their ability to find their way, to go long distances, and to time their travels reminds us how amazing nature can be. The fact that they live in different places at different times also illustrates the fascinating connections between creatures and their world.

❧ It's important to realize that there are still lots of things we can learn from and about our nonhuman neighbors. It's also important to keep in mind all of their needs in the places they call home. By considering the impact our actions have on the environment and its wild creatures, we can help ensure the future health and beauty of this amazing world, this world of wonder.

NATURE NOTE: *The ruddy turnstone, a bird that nests on the Arctic tundra and winters in the southern hemisphere, can fly 600 miles (960 km) in a single day.*

Fall migrations fill the sky with birds

WORDS TO KNOW

An **adaptation** is a characteristic or behavior that contributes to a living thing's ability to survive or reproduce.

The world is divided into a northern **hemisphere** and southern hemisphere by the equator.

The young of some animals that change from one form to another as they develop are called **larvae**.

Lichens are organisms made up of algae and fungi living together. They provide valuable food for caribou.

The earth's **magnetic field** is an invisible characteristic of the planet that causes compass needles to point north.

When an insect goes through **metamorphosis**, it changes from one developmental stage to another.

Navigation is the process of finding the way from one place to another.

Phytoplankton are tiny plants that float in the ocean and other bodies of water.

A large, treeless expanse of land found in the far North is called a **tundra**.

Zooplankton are tiny animals that float in the ocean and other bodies of water.

INDEX